Pope Francis

Man of Peace

REV. JUDE WINKLER, OFM Conv.

Imprimi Potest: Very Rev. James McCurry, OFM Conv., Minister Provincial of Our Lady of the Angels Province (USA)
Nihil Obstat: Rev. Msgr. James M. Cafone, M.A., S.T.D., Censor Librorum
Imprimatur: ✠ **Most Rev. John J. Myers, J.C.D., D.D.**, Archbishop of Newark

The Nihil Obstat and Imprimatur are official declarations that a book or pamphlet is free of doctrinal or moral error. No implication is contained therein that those who have granted the Nihil Obstat and Imprimatur agree with the contents, opinions or statements expressed.

Printed in China   CPSIA   February 2015   10 9 8 7 6 5 4 3 2 1 L/P

ISBN 978-1-941243-19-0

We Have Good News

AT 7 p.m. on March 13, 2013, a huge crowd that had gathered in St. Peter's Square in front of St. Peter's Basilica looked up at a small chimney and noticed that the smoke coming out was not black as it had been four times in the prior couple of days. Black smoke meant that the Cardinals meeting inside had not yet elected a new Pope. This time the smoke was white, a sign that the Holy Spirit had led the Cardinals to choose a new Pope for the Church.

A great gathering of people was already in the square, but with the white smoke, people flocked there from all over Rome. People stopped what they were doing all around the world to find out who had been elected as the new Pope.

Shortly afterward, a Cardinal came out onto the balcony and announced that there was good news: we had a Pope. He then announced his name. The new Pope was Cardinal Jorge Bergoglio from Argentina. He was the first Cardinal from the Americas ever to be elected Pope.

The Cardinal also announced that Cardinal Bergoglio had chosen the name Francis, a name never before selected by a Pope.

3

Born in Argentina

POPE Francis greeted the crowd by saying that it was the duty of the Cardinals to elect a new Pope. He told them that this time, they had gone to the ends of the earth to find one.

The new Pope was from a distant land: the city of Buenos Aires in Argentina. He was born there on December 17, 1936. His father had been born in Italy, and his mother had been born in Argentina (although her parents also had come from Italy). He grew up speaking both Spanish, the language spoken in Argentina, and Italian, the language of his ancestors.

Little Jorge Bergoglio was like many boys. He liked to play soccer. Even today, he continues to pay his dues to a soccer club in Argentina. He liked music and dancing. He was especially close to his Grandma Rosa who lived nearby. To this day, he still keeps a copy of the special prayer that she would say each day for her grandchildren.

When he was a teenager, his father found a job for him in a sock factory. It was not so much that the family needed the money, but rather that his father wanted to teach him responsibility, a lesson that he learned well.

God Touches His Heart

ONE day, Jorge was on his way to the train station to meet some friends. It was a holiday called Student Day, which marked the beginning of spring in Argentina. On his way, he decided to stop in a church and go to Confession. Something happened during that Confession that changed his life.

Jorge experienced the mercy of God in a way that he never had before. He was so moved by what had happened that he stayed in the church to pray and did not even go to meet his friends.

At just seventeen years of age, he knew that God was calling him to a special vocation. He wanted to serve God and God's people, and he especially wanted to share some of the love of God that he had felt that day in the confessional. The rest of his life he would tell people about God's mercy.

He deeply felt the mercy of God again when he was twenty-one and seriously ill. He had to have part of his lung removed, and the operation he had to undergo was very painful. He found consolation, however, in the words of a Sister who had taught him when he was very young. She would tell him, "You are imitating Christ."

Service as a Jesuit

JORGE continued his studies until he received a degree in chemistry. Yet, he knew that he was being called to be a Priest, and he continued to pray to know exactly how he was to live out his vocation.

He decided that God was calling him to join the Jesuit Order. The Jesuits were founded in the 1500s by St. Ignatius of Loyola. They are famed for their great learning and their talent for founding and running schools and universities. Since the days of St. Ignatius, they also preach a special thirty-day retreat for people to find the Will of God in their lives.

There were three things that attracted Jorge to the Jesuits. The first was that they have a missionary spirit. Some of the first Jesuits traveled all the way to India, China, and Japan as missionaries.

The second thing that he liked about the Jesuits is that they live in community. Even today, Pope Francis has chosen to live in the midst of a larger community so that he can meet and talk with people.

Finally, Jorge liked their discipline. Jesuits take a vow of obedience, and many make a special promise of obedience to the Holy Father.

Difficult and Dangerous Times

ONE of Jorge's first jobs as a Jesuit was to teach in a high school. His students liked him because he always treated each of them with respect.

Ordained a Priest in 1969, Jorge was soon asked to be the novice master for his community. This means that he would take care of the young men who were entering the Jesuits and deciding whether this truly was God's call in their lives.

In 1973, he was chosen as the Provincial for the Jesuits in Argentina and Uruguay. A Provincial is the man who is in charge of all of the Jesuits living in a certain area. He was very young for this work, but he did his best and trusted in God's mercy.

These were difficult years in Argentina. The military had taken over the government, and they were fighting people whom they felt were terrorists. Both sides kidnapped and killed many innocent people.

Father Jorge risked his life to protect some of those innocent people. He hid them in one of the schools he was running. More than that, he gave one of them who looked like him his proof of identity so that he might escape the country before he was killed.

Called to Be a Bishop

WHEN Father Jorge finished his time as Provincial, he went to Germany to study. Afterward, he served as the head of a Jesuit seminary. He also wrote some books to help other religious live their special calling.

On May 13, 1992, he had a meeting with the Papal Nuncio (the Pope's ambassador) to Argentina. They talked about many different things, and, at the end of the conversation, the Nuncio told him that he had one more thing to tell him: he had just been named the Auxiliary Bishop of Buenos Aires.

As a Jesuit, Father Jorge knew that he was not to seek any kind of office within the Church; he was not to look for promotions. Still, he had taken a vow of obedience to the Holy Father, and this was something he could not refuse.

As soon as he became a Bishop, he decided that his ministry would be one of mercy. He took a special saying for his motto: "Seeing through the eyes of mercy, he chose him." This is what the Gospels say about Jesus' choice to call St. Matthew as an Apostle, and Bishop Jorge knew this was true for himself as well.

Serving the Poor

FIVE years later, Bishop Jorge had another meeting with the same Papal Nuncio. They were having an ordinary meal when he noticed that someone had brought in a cake and some champagne. He wondered whether it was the Nuncio's birthday, but there was another reason for the celebration. The Pope had decided that Bishop Jorge was to become the Archbishop of Buenos Aires.

Even when he was Archbishop, he continued to act in a very humble way. He asked people to call him Father Jorge. He did not live in a big building, but rather in a small apartment. He cooked meals for himself and for his guests. He refused to be driven in a fancy car; he would take the bus like everyone else.

He had a special love for the poor. He would visit the worst sections of the city and spend time with people who felt that no one loved them or cared for them. He wore a silver cross around his neck as a sign of him being a Bishop. That cross quickly became tarnished from the kisses and tears from the poor people whom he met. He invited other Priests to reach out to the poor and to serve them with love and kindness.

Two Popes

IN 2001, Pope John Paul II appointed Archbishop Jorge a Cardinal of the Church. Cardinals advise the Holy Father and also elect a new Pope when the previous one either dies or resigns.

In 2005, Pope John Paul II, who is now a Saint of the Church, died after a long illness. This was the first time that Cardinal Jorge took part in a Conclave. A Conclave is a gathering of all of the Cardinals from all over the world who are under 80 years of age. They close the doors to the Sistine Chapel where they stay and dedicate themselves to prayer and listening to the voice of the Holy Spirit.

This time, the Cardinals very quickly elected Cardinal Ratzinger to be the new Pope. He took the name of Benedict, and he was the sixteenth Pope to choose that name.

In February 2013, Pope Benedict was meeting with some of the Cardinals. At the end of that meeting, the Pope made a surprise announcement: he was going to resign at the end of the month. This had not happened for a long, long time. People all over the world were shocked. Yet, they all understood that the demands of being Pope had affected his health.

Pope Francis

ONCE again, the Cardinals met in Rome and for several days, they discussed Church matters and learned more about each other as they prepared to elect a new Pope.

At the end of their discussions, they closed themselves in their Conclave and began to vote for the new Pope. On the fifth ballot, Cardinal Jorge Bergoglio was elected as the new Pope. One of his friends, a Cardinal from Brazil, was sitting next to him. When he congratulated him, he told the new Pope always to remember the poor.

This was one of the reasons why the new Pope chose the name Francis. He wanted to name himself after St. Francis of Assisi. St. Francis had chosen to live a life of poverty so that he could live as Jesus did when He was upon the earth. He also wanted to live like the poor because he knew that God loved them in a special way.

St. Francis also was a man of peace. He helped people to forgive each other and to live in peace. Pope Francis wanted to bring that same peace to our times. He knew that the only way that he could do that was to love everyone just like God loves them.

Simple Acts

ONE of the ways that he would teach people about the love of Jesus was to give them a good example. As soon as he was elected, he continued his practice of not being driven in a fancy car. He asked those in charge of cars at the Vatican to let him use a simple car.

He very quickly realized that there were poor people who were being ignored and even hurt by others. Among them were people who had fled from their own country either because of war or because they were so poor that they could not even feed their children. He visited camps where these people were being kept and asked those in charge to treat them with dignity.

Once, when his car was taking him around St. Peter's Square, he had the driver stop so that he could bless a man who was paralyzed. Again, he was teaching us that no one should ever be ignored or treated badly just because he was different.

On his first Holy Thursday as Holy Father, he decided not to celebrate Mass at the Basilica of St. John Lateran in Rome. Instead, he visited a number of young people who were being held in prison.

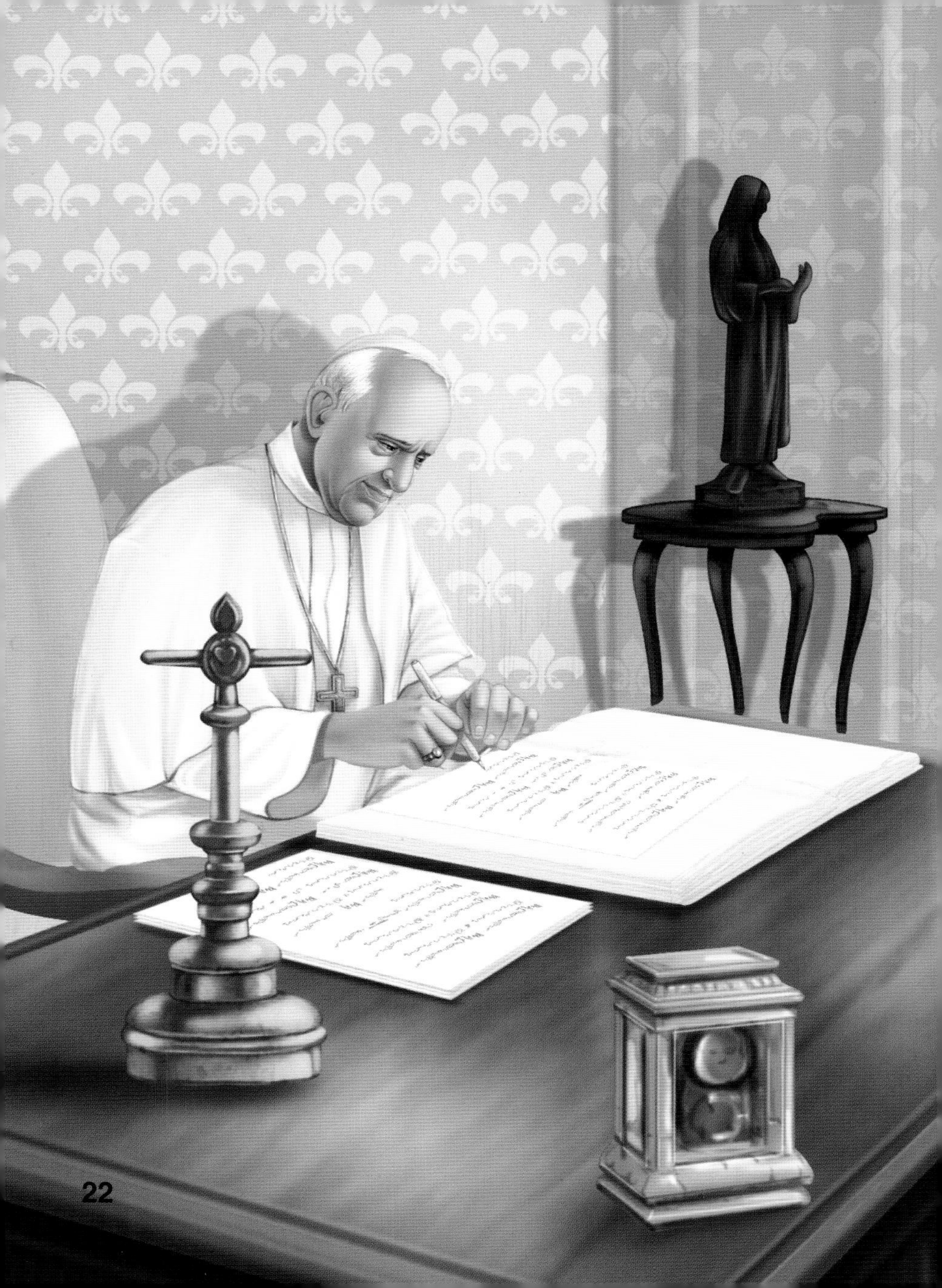

The God of Mercy

MOVED as he was by God's mercy, Pope Francis kept as Pope the motto he had as a Bishop. He wants to share the message of mercy that he had experienced deeply so many years before in the confessional—and which he felt called to proclaim all throughout his priesthood. He told all the Priests around the world to be merciful when they listen to Confessions.

One of the ways that he has shared God's mercy is by answering some of the letters that he receives. So many people write to the Holy Father that he would never have time to answer all the letters. While he has some people who read through the letters and write an answer for him, he decided that some of the letters needed his personal touch.

The Pope called one unmarried woman who was going to have a baby. Her boyfriend was against the birth, but she decided that the baby was God's gift whose life she must protect. The Holy Father called her to encourage her and to tell her that he was praying for her. He also told her that she could bring the baby to St. Peter's Basilica and he himself would celebrate the child's Baptism.

Be Filled with Hope

HE also speaks to many young people about their future. He had taught in a high school and worked with university students. He knows that young people want to hear a message of truth from someone who believes and lives his words.

The Pope calls upon them to be people of hope. He wants them to shape a future in which the message of Jesus will be lived with enthusiasm. He tells them of his confidence in them and his prayers for them.

He reminds them that God is calling them to a vocation. Some of them will be called to marriage and some to become Priests or Religious. He tells them that they should be willing to commit themselves to their calling for the rest of their lives.

Pope Francis wrote a special letter to people all around the world called *The Joy of the Gospel*. In it, he tells us that if we really want to share the Gospel with others, we are to do so filled with the joy of true Christians. This joy is not nonstop fun or laughter, but it is a joy that is to replace any anger or sadness we may feel. The Pope points out that true joy comes from living in God's love and sharing it with others, especially by serving them.

A Church Giving Witness

HE also has called upon Catholics all over the world to live what we say we are. Sometimes we can give a bad example to others by going to church on Sunday but then the rest of the week not living like Christ did. No one will believe what we say if we do not live it. So Pope Francis keeps reminding us that the Gospel has to change the way we think and act. We have to follow Jesus' example of loving and serving everyone around us.

The Pope is preaching this message to everybody in the Church, including Cardinals and Bishops and Priests and Sisters. He wants those who lead the Church to be the first to give the example of living a life of humble service to others.

He told a group of Priests one Holy Thursday that Jesus called them to be the shepherds of the Church, so they should smell a little like the sheep. What he was saying is that they should not be afraid to get their hands dirty in serving those who need their help and their love. He reminded them that, for Christians, the person who is most important is the one who is willing to wash other people's feet, just like Jesus did at the Last Supper.

A Man of Prayer

ONE of the things that those who know Pope Francis tell us is that he is a man of prayer. This is something that was clear from the first moments that he was named Pope. When he came out on the balcony to give his first message to those gathered in St. Peter's Square and those watching all throughout the world, he did two important things.

He first of all said an Our Father, a Hail Mary, and a Glory Be for Pope Benedict. He then bowed his head and asked for people to pray for him before he gave all of us his blessing.

Pope Francis gets up early in the morning to begin his prayers. He prays the Psalms, meditates, celebrates Mass, and prays the Rosary. All throughout the day, whenever there is a small period of time, he tries to return to his prayers so that everything he says and does will be filled with the grace of God. Then, in the evening, he spends an hour in adoration before the Blessed Sacrament, which is one of his favorite types of prayer.

He even has invited the leaders of peoples who are fighting each other to join him in prayer at the Vatican. He realizes that it is only by calling upon God that we can solve our problems here on earth.

His Favorite Saints

POPE Francis also knows that we will not be able to change without the help of our heavenly intercessors, the Saints.

The Pope especially loves and prays to the Blessed Virgin Mary. One of his favorite images of Mary is one that he first saw in Germany when he was studying there. It is called "Mary, the Untier of Knots." We often get so caught up in what is happening that we believe that we cannot find a way out of our difficulties. Mary is there to help us find a solution so that we can be free to make the right choices.

He loves St. Francis, the Poor Man of Assisi. He is basing his service as Holy Father upon the example of this humble Saint. He realizes that one does not have to be powerful to give a powerful witness.

Pope Francis also has great love for St. Thérèse of Lisieux. She spoke about the fact that most of us will never be given the chance to do truly great things. Yet, she believed that all of us can do small things with great love. The Pope has said, "Whenever I have a problem, I ask her not to resolve it, but to take it in her hands and help me accept it, and as a sign, I almost always receive a white rose."

A Prayer for the Pope

THE Holy Spirit has called Pope Francis to lead the Church. When he first became Pope, he asked us to pray for him. Therefore, let us pray:

Loving and merciful God,
Please send Your Spirit of Holiness into the heart of
    Pope Francis.
Let him be gentle and humble like the Saint after
    whom he is named.
Let him be granted a long life of love and service in
    Your name.
And, most of all, let him continue to challenge us to
    be better Christians,
To live what we say we are. Amen.